IMAGINATION STRETCHERS

By
Liz & Dick Wilmes
Art
Donna Dane

A **BUILDING BLOCKS** Publication

3893 Brindlewood, Elgin, Illinois 60120

ISBN 0-943452-04-x
Library of Congress Catalog No. 85-071414

COVER CONSULTANTS:
Pat and Greg Samata
Samata Associates, Inc.
Dundee, Illinois 60118

GRAPHIC ASSISTANT:
Jennifer Dobbins

ABOUT THE ARTIST:
Donna Dane is a multi-talented freelance illustrator. Throughout the past several years she has worked with BUILDING BLOCKS on many of our newspaper issues and has illustrated both THE CIRCLE TIME BOOK and FELT BOARD FUN. She lives with her husband Bruce and two children Rachel and Joshua in Southern California. Her son Joshua is given credit for the cover concept of IMAGINATION STRETCHERS.

PUBLISHED BY:
BUILDING BLOCKS
3893 Brindlewood
Elgin, Illinois 60120

DISTRIBUTED BY:
GRYPHON HOUSE, Inc.
P.O. Box 275
Mt. Ranier, Maryland 20712

ISBN 0-943452-04-X
>> $6.95 <<

DEDICATED TO:

. . . those little seeds of great thoughts.

Contents

Introduction

Most children enjoy talking, especially when they are given encouragement, when they are discussing something with which they are familiar, and/or when they are sure that other people are listening. IMAGINATION STRETCHERS has been written primarily for adults to use while helping young children learn and strengthen their language skills. As you use the stretchers, you'll notice these language skills develop. Through the stretchers, the children will learn to:

- Express their ideas.
- Expand their vocabulary.
- Enhance their listening skills.
- Think beyond their first several thoughts.
- Become more alert to their environment.
- Develop the ability to sequence.
- Role play situations.
- Appreciate other people's ideas.

Using Imagination Stretchers

IMAGINATION STRETCHERS contains a wide variety of conversation starters. As you use the different ideas, you'll become more familiar with:

- Riddles, questions, and statements which have hundreds of correct responses and no wrong ones.
- Rhymes which provoke additional thought.
- Situations which occur in young children's everyday world.
- Challenges which tease the brain.
- Observations which can be expanded and expanded and expanded.

IMAGINATION STRETCHERS is divided by months. Each section contains between thirty-three and thirty-five stretchers, so that you can enjoy one or more everyday. You'll notice that each month begins with several holidays. Try to use these holiday stretchers before, during, and after the celebration. The conversations you will have with the children will help them to better understand specific holidays, get a 'feel' for holidays in general, and create new and exciting ways to celebrate these special days.

In addition to using the holiday stretchers at appropriate times, use the other stretchers throughout the month. You can go about this in several different ways. For example, select one or two stretchers each morning that you would like to use that day. When you have several extra moments with the children or when the opportunity presents itself, share the stretcher and let the conversation begin. Another way is to read through all of the stretchers for the month and use them as they become appropriate each day.

Think! Think! Think!

Children will need time and probably some encouragement to think. Ideas will not necessarily come 'pouring out' immediately. A child may create several, you may think of several more and then you will both run out of ideas. Now comes the additional excitement inherent to each stretcher — the challenge of continuing to stretch your imaginations. You and the children may think of more ideas that day, maybe several days later a thought will 'pop' into your heads, or additional ideas may surprise you several weeks later when you least expect them. Share all of these with each other. Listen to the children and encourage them as they share their ideas with you.

Besides time, children need support as they stretch their imaginations. You can give them this encouragement in a variety of ways:
- Through 'setting the stage' for the stretcher by:
  - Using it when something in the environment makes it a natural, such as when a bird flies overhead you can say, *"What could that bird be thinking about?"*
  - Creating a short story which leads into the stretcher.
  - Reflecting on things the children have recently done which relate to the stretcher you're going to use.
  - Going for a real or imaginary walk which will relate to the stretcher.
  - Saying, *"Let's put on our thinking caps. I've got a riddle we'll enjoy thinking about."*
  - Continually presenting the children with information and thoughts which they can use as background for other stretchers.
- Through phrases like:
  - *"That's using your brain!"*
  - *"Good idea. Let's think of another one."*
  - *"You just said . . . . . "* (repeat the child's idea)
  - *"Your idea makes me think of . . . . . "* (add an idea)
  - *"Let's see."* (pause for the child to think)
  - *"This morning we began thinking about . . . . . Have you thought of any more ideas?"*
- Through body language such as:
  - Smiling.
  - Pointing to their head.
  - Shaking their hand.
  - Hugging them.
  - Flashing them the A-OK sign.
- Through urgings such as:
  - Asking the children to repeat their thoughts.
  - Listing aloud all the ideas you and the children have created to that point about a certain topic.
  - Letting the children whisper their thoughts to you and then you say them aloud for everyone to hear.
  - Implementing ideas they create, so they can see how ideas carry over into action.

'Stretching' With Emily

As you read through the following excerpts from a conversation we recently had with a young child, you'll recognize how we use several of the above suggestions.

Dick and I went to lunch the other day with a good friend of ours, Emily. She is four years old and lives in Dundee, Illinois with her mom, dad, and sister, Jillian. It was a beautiful spring afternoon in the middle of May. We went to a small restaurant located right on the Fox River. There, we sat at a table by the window so we could watch the river.

Our first opportunity for a stretcher occurred when a mama duck and her babies came swimming down the river.

Adult: *"Look outside, Emily! Can you see that duck with her babies? How many babies? Can you count them real fast?"*

Emily: *"One, two, three, four, five."* (There were really six.)

Adult: *"Five babies. They look like they were just born. Why do you think they are swimming so close to their mom?"*

Emily: *"They don't want to get lost."*

Adult: *"Do you really think they could get lost? Why?"*

Emily: *"Because they are so tiny."*

Adult: *"Any other reason they would want to be close to their mommy?"*

Emily: *"They love her."*

Adult: *"Oh, they love her."*

(At this point the ducks disappeared into the weeds and we began talking about something else.)

Adult: *"Oh, Emily, there go the baby ducks with their mama."*

Emily: *"Maybe they are looking for food."*

Adult: *"That could be another reason the babies stay close to their mom."*

Emily: *"Yeh! They eat little, tiny fish and everything."*

Adult: *"Oh. Where do they get the fish?"*

Emily: *"In the water."*

Adult: *"I don't see any fish."*

Emily: *"The mama goes under the water."*

(There was another pause in the conversation.)

Adult: *"Here comes the mama duck again with one, two babies. Oh, there are the rest. Can you see them? Look way down. The babies look like they are running away."*

Emily: *"Why are those little ducks trying to run away?"*

Adult: *"Yeh, why would those ducks want to run away? I thought they were going to stay real close to their mom. We'll have to watch. They all went back into the weeds."*

Emily: *"Why?"*

Adult: *"What could they do there?"*

Emily: *"Maybe play."*

Adult: *"Yeh!"*

(Several minute pause.)

Adult: *"See the baby ducks. What are they doing?"*

Emily: *"They are running away again."*

Adult: *"They are in front of their mom."*

Emily: *"Maybe she's teaching them."*

Adult: *"She wants to teach them. That's another reason the ducks could stay close. They are learning something."*

CONVERSATION II

Emily, Dick, and I talked about so many things during lunch. As we were finishing, the ducks prompted another stretcher.

Emily: *"Look, ducks can fly."*

Adult: *"Yeh, ducks can fly. Ducks can swim and ducks can fly. What other things can fly?"*

Emily: *"Airplanes, rocketships. They turn and go straight up."*

Adult: *"Ducks can fly. Airplanes can fly. Rocketships can fly."* (Pause)

Emily: *"I can't think of anything else."*

Adult: *"I can think of a couple more. I think, kites. What have we thought of so far?"*

Emily: (Ignoring my question) *"Birds, balloons!"*

10

Adult: *"Bats can fly."*

Emily: *"Yuck!"*

Adult: *"They might be yuck, but they can fly. I can think of one more. It's real big. It has lots of colors. It flies over Dundee sometimes."*

Emily: *"What colors?"*

Adult: *"Blue, red, green."*

Emily: *"A hot air balloon? I never saw that over Dundee. I saw it over Illinois."*

Adult: *"You've seen one in Illinois!"*

Emily: *"Clouds fly."*

Adult: *"I'm trying to think of other things that fly."*

Emily: *"Me, too."*

Adult: *"Superman."*

Emily: (Laughing) *"He isn't real."*

Adult: *"I've 'gotta' think of one more."* (Pause) *"I know, a bee."*

Emily: *"The only thing I can think of is a helicopter."*

Adult: *"Oh, you figured one out, too."*

Emily: *"Arrows."*

Adult: *"Arrows. Do arrows fly by themselves?"*

Emily: *"Do you remember the Indians? They shoot arrows, remember?"*

Adult: *"With their bow?"*

Emily: *"Are you thinking of another one?"*

Adult: *"I'm still thinking."*

Emily: **So am I.**

It was time for us to go and we had leisurely exhausted all of our ideas. We asked Emily to call us if she thought of any later that day and we would do the same. She did think of two more as were were driving home—leaves in the wind and dandelion puffs.

JANUARY

NEW YEARS DAY celebrates the beginning of each new year. Start by developing a new habit. Towards the end of the day, say this chant to your child, let him think and then share some of his favorite happenings of the day.

Eric, Eric what do you say?
What were the best things about today?
      Dick Wilmes

If you could do whatever you wanted all day long, what would you do?

What new things would you like to learn about?

DR. MARTIN LUTHER KING, JR.'S BIRTHDAY honors a man who spent his life searching for peace among all people. If a new child moves into your neighborhood, how would you make him feel welcome?

Two friends want to play with the same toy. How can they solve their problem peacefully?

Read this rhyme to your child and then make lots of wishes.

I WISH

Way up in the sky at night
I see the stars so big and bright.
I wish and hope those stars could bring
This very, very special thing.
Dick Wilmes

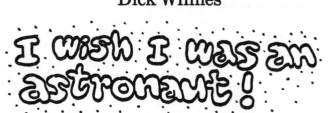

CHINESE NEW YEAR begins the new year for the Chinese people. Red symbolizes happiness to the Chinese people. Talk about colors which make you happy.
EXTENSION: Do some colors make you feel warm or cold? Why do you like certain colors?

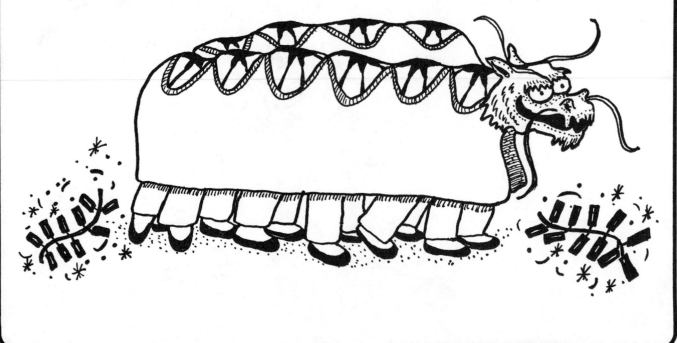

Why are balloons so much fun?

What kinds of cereal are there?

If you could look beyond the stars, what do you think you would see?

What can you buy in a bakery?

Pretend you're playing. What would you be doing?

Guess what's in my purse.

Pretend you're Jack Frost and you're going to paint ice pictures on everyone's windows. What kinds of pictures will you create?

Do you ever lose your mittens? What could you do so you always know where they are?

Bring a bucket of snow into the house. Have your child wear mittens and enjoy playing with it inside. What is happening to the snow? Why?

You want to go sledding, but you don't have a sled. What else could you use?

JANUARY

Talk aloud to yourself, but within hearing distance of your child. *"OK, I need to plan what to have for dinner. Let's see, we can have pork chops and peas. What else can we have? Sara help me out. Open the cabinet (refrigerator) and see what else we can have."*

Read this rhyme and then discover all of the things your fingers can do.

TEN FINGERS

These are my ten fingers.
They do whatever I say.
They help me when I'm eating.
They help me when I play.

Sometimes they work together.
Sometimes they work apart.
Your fingers can do so many
*   things.*
Can you think of one to start?
        Dick Wilmes

After you have enjoyed this quiet rhyme with your child, talk about dreams you each have had.

GOOD NIGHT

The little candle burns so bright,
It lights a corner of the night.
The flame is hot I'm sure you know.
To turn it off you simply blow.
Wh-h-h-h Good Night!
        Dick Wilmes

Have cheese chunks and stick pretzels. Pretend they are tinker toys. Build your snack and then enjoy it.

If you lost your mittens, how would you keep your hands warm?

What do you know about snow? EXTENSION: Cut a snowflake.

What toys can you fit in your pocket?

Round, round, what is round?

As your child is watching a television program ask him, *"What do you like about what you are watching?"*

Name your toys that have wheels.

Playing with balls is usually an outside activity, but oh, they are so much fun. What can you do with balls inside? Have fun!

Pretend it is a very hot day. You've decided to go to the beach to keep cool. Talk about what you are going to take. Toys? A picnic lunch? Clothes?

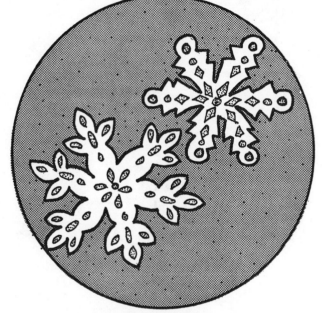

JANUARY

What things do you need help with?

It's cold when snow goes down your back. How are you going to keep it out? Try one of your ideas next time you play in the snow.

Give your child a cylinder-shaped box. Ask him *"What could you do with this?"*
EXTENSION: After your child has finished playing with it, give him some art supplies and scrap materials so he can create an animal, vehicle, or design. Discuss his creation when finished. Maybe use it for a centerpiece on the kitchen table.

Make different noises with your shoes.
EXTENSION: Have your child trace his shoes and then paint the tracings with watercolors.

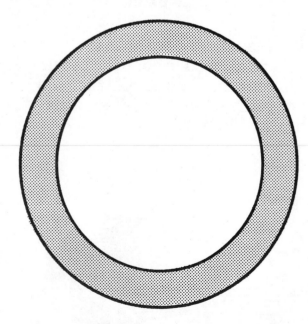

What could this be a picture of?

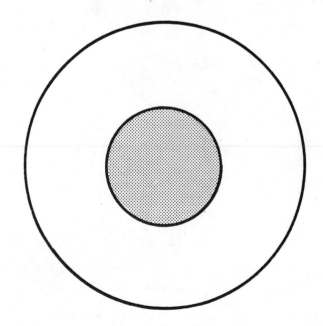

What does this remind you of?

FEBRUARY

HOLIDAYS

GROUND HOG DAY features the ground hog who helps predict when spring weather will begin. Just as the ground hog looks for his shadow, look for yours at different times of the day.

Find your shadow. Who has a shadow bigger than yours? Maybe an elephant?

Ground hogs are vegetarians. What are your favorite vegetables?

Carrots crunch as you chew them. What other vegetables go *crunch, crunch, crunch* as you eat?

VALENTINES DAY celebrates love. How do you show someone that you love him?

You've just used your last piece of red paper and you have three more valentines to make. What are you going to use to make them?

To whom would you like to send valentines?

Be alert for red objects.

Think about all of the reasons you are special.

PRESIDENTS' DAY celebrates the birthdays of two presidents, George Washington and Abraham Lincoln. Have a birthday party. Decorate with flags and have red, white, and blue foods and drinks. What will you serve?

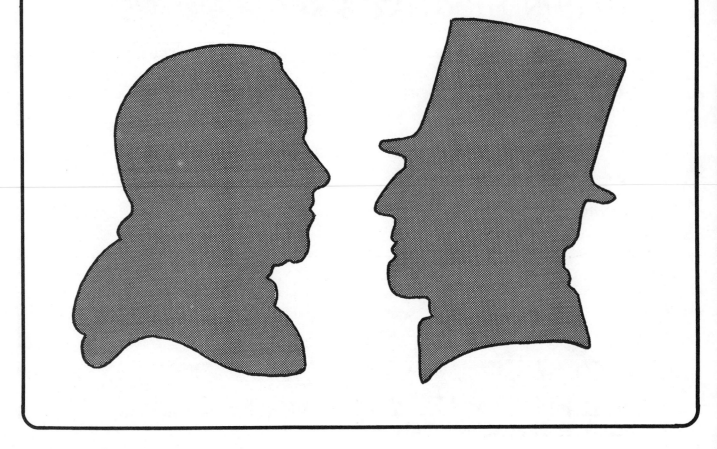

What kind of toys do you play with in the snow?

What things could you use to make tracks in the snow?
EXTENSION: Read *A Snowy Day* by Ezra Jack Keats.

Think of all of the words that describe how you feel when you're sick.

Pretend your hand is a mirror. Hold it in front of your face. What do you see?

All of the doors in your car are locked and the keys are in the ignition. What can you do? Think of all of the possibilities.

What kinds of animals would you like to have for pets? Why? What would be fun about each pet?

How many ways can you think of to melt an ice cube?

Let your child enjoy playing with several pipe cleaners.

What toppings can you put on a pizza?
EXTENSION: Try some new toppings the next time you have a pizza.

FEBRUARY

Read this rhyme and then think about what you do while you are eating popcorn.

EZ POPPER

Take a little oil.
Take a little seed.
Put them in a popper,
And heat is all you need.
                    Dick Wilmes

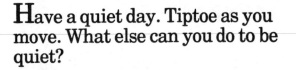

Have a quiet day. Tiptoe as you move. What else can you do to be quiet?

How do you know when someone likes you?

If you were going to color the snow, what would you use?

It is cold outside and the heat is not working in your home. How are you going to stay warm? Read this rhyme for one clue.

WINTER WIND

The winter wind is cold outside.
The snow is whirling 'round.
So under the covers my head I'll hide
And never make a sound.
                    Dick Wilmes

Walk around your house and see how many different smells you can find.
EXTENSION: Put various items, such as soap, talcum powder, and chocolate, in paper cups. Cover them and then try to identify each of them by their smell.

Several hours before bath time, put two trays on the counter. Have your child find objects around the house that he thinks will sink or float. Put the 'sink' objects on one tray and the 'float' objects on the other tray. Let your child try them in the bath water.

How many ways can you think of to scoop peanut butter out of a jar?

Make three wishes for yourself.

Have a POINT OUT GOOD DAY. On your P.O.G. day, tell as many people as you can what you like about them.

If you wanted to make a baby smile and giggle how would you do it?

You begin walking down the sidewalk and you notice that it is very slippery. What will you do?

MARCH

HOLIDAYS

FIRST DAY OF SPRING begins a new season. The spring wind is great for kite flying. What else is the wind good for? EXTENSION: Enjoy this rhyme and then fly a kite.

KITES

The wind blew gently across the ground
The kite began to fly.
I held onto the string and pulled
As it rose into the sky.

Higher than my mother's head
Higher than the tree.
Up to where the airplanes fly
And all controlled by me.
                    Dick Wilmes

Close your eyes and picture a baby animal. How does it move? Think of another animal. How does it move? Keep thinking of different animals.

Think about baby animals. Name the ones that you think would be soft, furry, and cuddly.

What are all of the things you need to help a flower grow?

PASSOVER is a Jewish festival of freedom. The Afrikkomen (a special piece of Matzah bread) brings 'good luck' to the person who finds it. What does 'good luck' mean?

Each home is thoroughly cleaned to prepare for the Passover celebration. If you were going to clean your room very, very well, what are all of the things you'd have to do?

ST. PATRICK'S DAY commemorates one of the greatest Irish heroes. When you think of the color green, what do you think about?

Read this rhyme and try to figure out all of the places that Wee Little Patrick might have gone.

WEE LITTLE PATRICK

*Patrick is a leprechaun.
He has a sack of gold.
He hides it in a special place
Between two stumps I'm told.*

*I think I once saw Patrick
Out in the woods at play
He smiled and laughed and winked his eye,
And then he ran away.*

*Don't try to follow Patrick
To find his treasure sack
He'll twist and jump and run away
And never will come back.*
                    Dick Wilmes

Some people think there is gold in a leprechaun's pot. What else could be in it?

Using construction paper, cut out several simple shapes—squares, triangles, circles—for your child. Let him enjoy arranging them in various designs and configurations. Listen as he talks to himself. Pick up on any cues he may give you to extend his conversation.

What can you do with a piece of bread?

Pretend you have a long neck like the giraffe. What new things might you see?

What do you have around your house that you could stack together or put on top of each other? Do you have blocks? Poker chips? Look in your cabinets, maybe you'll find something else.

There's a song that begins, *"Bend and stretch, reach for the stars..."*. What else could you reach for? Substitute your words in the song and enjoy singing.

The March winds are blowing very hard and you left your bedroom windows open. When you go into the room, what will be blown around? Think hard. Did you have anything on your dresser? Are your stuffed friends still sitting on the bed?

What's the sun good for?

Pick a number from 1-10. Look for groups of that number as you walk through the grocery store. For example, you pick number 3. You might see 3 loaves of bread, 3 bananas in a bunch, 3 boxes of cereal in a row, and so on.

Look at and think about the different parts of your body. What shapes do you find? Start with your face, then go to your arm. It's fun and you'll be surprised how many circles, triangles, squares, and rectangles you carry around with you everyday.

How do you feel when the wind is blowing very hard at your face?

What do you do when you are too cold?

MARCH

If you can't fall asleep what do you do?

Using your index and middle fingers, make a V shape. Look carefully at your V. What does the V shape look like? Maybe rabbit ears?

Name all of the things you can that are made from wood.

What are all of the things you can do with your nose?

What are your favorite things to do at home?

What things do you use to keep your hair clean and neat?

How are people like birds? Pretend you are a bird as you enjoy this rhyme.

BIRDS

If I were a bird
I would learn to fly
Twisting and turning
All over the sky.

Up to the cloud
Down to the ground
Stretching my wings
As I turned all around.

Come pretend and fly
With me
Up to our home
In the top of the tree.
      Dick Wilmes

28

Name all of the different pieces of furniture you have in your house.

What types of balls can you fit in your pocket?

Make a food with your child for which you must use an electric mixer to beat some of the ingredients. Talk about what the mixer sounds like.

Enjoy some arm dancing. Pick out two crayons, one for each hand. Have a large sheet of paper. Set the radio to a music station or play a musical record. Let your arms dance to the music and create a colorful design.
EXTENSION: If crayons and paper aren't available, simply let your arms dance to the music—great for travelling.

What are all of the different ways you could say *"Good Morning"* to your family?
EXTENSION: Each day during the next week, say *"Good Morning"* a different way.

Think of all of the things which feel soft.

APRIL

HOLIDAYS

APRIL FOOLS DAY is a day of silliness and playful tricks. Think of lots of silly sandwiches. What combinations did you create? Taste one, if you dare.

Look at this 'goofy' picture. Find all of the tricks.

EASTER is a Christian holiday celebrating the resurrection of Jesus. When He arose, He started talking to His friends. What do you think they talked about?

The Easter Bunny has run out of eggs and other goodies to give to the children. He still has five more families to visit and doesn't want to disappoint them. What can the Easter Bunny leave for these children?

What goodies do you think will be in your Easter basket?

ARBOR DAY recognizes the importance of conservation and preserving the environment, especially the forests. Take a walk to a nearby park or forest preserve. Rub your hand slowly on the barks of different trees. How do they feel? How do they smell?

What do you like about trees?
EXTENSION: Read Shel Silverstein's *The Giving Tree*.

APRIL

Why is it fun to play in the rain?

If you were outside and it began to rain, what would you do to keep dry?

What would you do if you went to your bedroom and your bed had disappeared?

How is the sky different when it's raining from when the sun is shining?

When people get angry at each other, what should they do?

WHAT DO YOU DO WHEN YOU'RE FRIGHTENED?

*What do you do when you're
    frightened?
Do you cry when you are sad?
A smile will show you're happy.
A frown that you are mad.*

*Our feelings are inside of us.
They're changing every day.
Sometimes we show them to each
    other
In our own very special way.*
                    Dick Wilmes

What letters can you make with your body?

32

What kinds of things can you buy at the grocery store?

How do birds know when to land?

How many ways can you sit on a chair?

Name all of the types of clothes that people wear. Keep thinking, there are lots of them.

Give your child the box of old crayons. Have him sort them into two piles—long ones and short ones. Next time maybe he can separate them by color.

What can you do in a puddle? EXTENSION: Can you do the same things in a swimming pool? Different things? What?

What makes loud noises?

If you had a whale for a pet, where could he live?

33

How do you know that it is Springtime?

Next time you're in the car, look around the inside and find all of the things that move. You won't believe it.

Do you have a rubberband handy? Take it out. How many different directions can you stretch it? Do any of your shapes look like objects that you recognize? What?

Why do you like books?

Name different things you sit on such as a chair or a picnic bench.

What's fun about a library?

What do you do when you're scared? How about other feelings?

Blow a dandelion and make a wish for someone else. Wish again and again.

What foods do you put in your toaster?

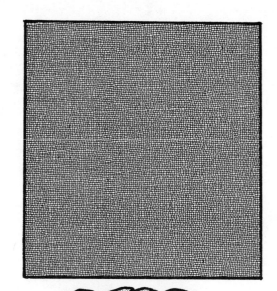

APRIL

Put a piece of sandpaper, felt, cotton, or corduroy on this square. How does it feel?

Read this rhyme and then figure out all of the reasons why babies cry.

MY BABY BROTHER IS CRYING

*My baby brother is crying
He cries an awful lot,
He cries when he is tired or wet.
He cries when he is not.*

*Sometimes when I am sleeping,
I hear him fuss and cry,
So Mom and Dad get out of bed
And check to find out why.*

*Babies have to cry you see
To let their parents know
When they are uncomfortable
And the things they need to grow.*
            Dick Wilmes

Create an ALL BY MYSELF list. Start with the line below and repeat *"All by myself"* after each skill.

*There are many things I can do
All by myself
I can _____
All by myself.*

*I can _____
All by myself.*

Continue on and on.

EXTENSION: If your child is beginning to read or can read and write, write the list and hang it for all to see.

MAY

HOLIDAYS

MAY DAY is a festival of flowers. Take a short trip to a local florist. Smell the different flowers. Do you like the odors? Buy a flower for a friend.

CINCO DE MAYO is an important Mexican holiday celebrating victory over French soldiers. Breaking open a pinata is a favorite Mexican game. What kinds of things could you put into a pinata? One of my favorites is a little car.

MOTHER'S DAY sets aside some time to let us remember special women in our lives. Think of a favorite woman in your life. What is special about her?

Pretend you're the Mommy. What do you do all day?

MEMORIAL DAY is an American holiday giving tribute to men and women who have died for the United States. What fruits could you put in a red, white, and blue salad?

MAY

If a car could talk, what would it say as it goes through a car wash?

What objects in your house make noise? Does your door creak when you open and close it? Does your water do 'thleeeeeeesh' when you turn on the faucet? Keep thinking!

Where do you go in a car?

What could you do with a tire, a ball, and a piece of rope?

Look carefully at a patch of grass. How many different things do you see?

Name as many animals as you can that are taller than you are.

Pair off with a friend. One person makes a pair of binoculars with his hands. He looks through them at a person, something in nature, or an object. Then he describes what he is looking at to his partner. After his partner guesses what is being described, they switch roles.

If you were a grasshopper, what places would you hop to?

38

Pretend you are as small as an ant. What special things could you do?

What does a giant eat for lunch?

Name all of the things you do when you get up in the morning.

If all of a sudden you were lost, what could you do?

Look for buildings and other structures being built. What do you think they are going to be? Why?
EXTENSION: Go back when they are finished and see if you guessed right.

April showers bring May flowers. What else do April showers bring?

What would you like to teach me today?

Look at the sky. What do you see?

How many ways can you make noise?
EXTENSION: Play *"Blast-off."* Count backwards from ten to zero. When you say *"Zero"* make a noise. Count again and make a different noise.

Read the first stanza of this rhyme to your child and together think of all of the vegetables you could plant. Then enjoy the rest of the rhyme.

VEGETABLE GARDEN

I have a special piece of land
Just outside my door.
It's going to be a garden,
With vegetables galore.

First I'll plant the carrots,
Which grow below the ground,
With bushy green tops above,
They easily can be found.

Next I'll put tomato plants
Which grow so very wide.
I'll stake them up to spread them
  out
So none of them will hide.

Also there'll be cucumbers.
These I'll plant in a mound,
So they can grow every which way
Right along the ground.

Finally there'll be potatoes,
These are funny too.
They grow on roots below the soil
To dig when the summer's
  through.

If you don't plant a garden,
I certainly wonder why.
If you don't grow your own
  vegetables,
Then each one you must buy.
                    Dick Wilmes

40

What do birds think about as they fly around?

What kinds of balls are there?

What animals make their homes in trees?

What can you use to take your doll for a ride?

What do you know about a tree?

How many ways do you prepare eggs?

Close your eyes. Pretend you're in your bedroom. How many types of paper are there in your room? Now take an imaginary walk into your bathroom. What kinds of paper do you see in there?

What does a smile mean?

What things do you have around your house that you can draw a picture with?
EXTENSION: Next time you make a birthday card for a friend, use several of your drawing tools.

41

JUNE

HOLIDAYS

FLAG DAY salutes the United States flag. Look for United States flags. Talk about where the flags were and then read this rhyme.

OUR FLAG

The flag is coming. We see it now,
It's red and blue and white.
With stars and stripes, it's held so high
It's such a wonderful sight.

We are proud to hold our faces up
And stand so straight and tall,
To place our hands upon our hearts
And pray for peace for all.
                    Dick Wilmes

Look for other things that are red, white, and blue.

FATHER'S DAY sets aside some time to let us remember special men in our lives. What is special about a man you like?

Pick one of your favorite men. What does he look like?

Read this rhyme and talk about chores you do with your dad.

HELPING MY DAD

I like to help my dad alot
To rake the lawn or dry a pot.
It doesn't matter what's to be done.
When we do it together,
It's always more fun!!
                    Dick Wilmes

FIRST DAY OF SUMMER is the beginning of hot

weather and lots of playtime. Begin a 'Summer Fun' chain. First cut 90 strips (about 1" by 6") of colored construction paper. Put them in an envelope. Sometime during each day tell an adult something special that you had fun doing that day. The adult writes it on one of the strips of paper and then the child can add it to his chain. Begin on the first day of summer. Add to it each day. At the end of the season, you'll have a diary of 'Summer Fun.'

EXTENSION: Save the chain and drape it on your Christmas tree, mantel, or door during the December holidays.

What do you do in your sandbox? Now read this rhyme and decide if you do some of the same things as the child who plays in his magic land.

MY SAND BOX

On sunny days I go to play
In a magic land not far away.
It's filled with sand for castles
*   fair*
Or streets that go just everywhere.
And in my truck the sand I load
To fill a hole just down the road.
To find the place is not too hard
It's out the door in my back yard.
                    Dick Wilmes

What do you like about Summertime?

What are all of the tools you need to clean your house?

Let your child give his doll a bath. Before the bath talk about all of the things he will need. When it's bathtime, have him gather all of the items and then wash the doll. Of course, return all the props after the bath is over.

What foods can you eat with your fingers?

Why is it fun to wake up in the morning?

What do you think water animals do for fun?

What do you do at a picnic?

What do you throw in a waste-basket?

How many ways can you cross a river?

Why do you think that some grass in a field is green and some is brown or yellow?

What comes to your mind when you think about the sun?

Where can you find water to play in?

LUNCHTIME!! Create your own sandwich combination. Yum!

JUNE

Read this jingle and figure out where the bug might have gone.

1,2,3

1,2,3 there's a bug on me.
Where did he go?
I don't know.

How can you keep a balloon in the air?

What do you think about as you're swaying back and forth on a swing?

It's fun to use a pail in the sand. Where else could you use a pail? EXTENSION: Try it in places you've never tried before. How did it work?

Where do you hear music?

Name as many animals as you can that live in the zoo.

What beverages do you drink?

What animals, insects, and bugs fly?

What parts of your body can you touch your nose to?

Take an imaginary trip. Start by saying *"If I were going on a trip, I'd visit the beach. While I am there, I'd see shells."* Continue the story. (Take more imaginary trips, say to the fire station, to the mountains, to the train station and so on.)

What can you wear on your feet?

Name all of the types of weather you can think of.

JULY

HOLIDAYS

FOURTH OF JULY is the day that people in the United States celebrate independence. What colors do you see in the fireworks?

Pretend you're a clown in a parade. What tricks would you do?

MOON DAY celebrates man's first landing on the moon. Lie in the grass and look at the moon for awhile. Tell someone else what you see.

Read this rhyme and then decide what you like about parades.

TOWN PARADE

The people are beside the street,
All standing in the sun.
I hear the noon whistle blowing,
The parade has just begun.

First I hear police cars,
Sirens going "Vrrrum, Vrrrum!"
Driving slowly up the street,
Trying to make some room.

Next there comes the ambulance
Yellow as it can be.
With the paramedics ready,
In case of emergency.

Followed by the fire trucks,
The horns and whistles scream.
And hanging all along the rail,
Is the proud firefighting team.

Now there comes the color guard,
Scouts are marching proud.
Carrying the flags we all know,
Presenting them to the crowd.

The motorcycle troop is next,
You can hear them roar and zoom.
As they weave and turn about,
There hardly's any room.

Soon we see a tiny car,
Putting up the street.
Out jumps fourteen clowns,
Each with great big feet.

Don't forget the bands and such,
Making music fine.
Drums and horns and cymbals
    play,
All marching in a line.

There are floats that carry people,
A car to drive the queen.
People riding horseback,
And a street sweeping machine.

Finally comes the last police car,
The music starts to fade.
We had a nice afternoon,
Watching the town parade.
                        Dick Wilmes

49

If you were a little fish and a giant fish was going to eat you, what would you do?
EXTENSION: Read *Swimmy* by Leo Lionni.

Name the utensils you use in the kitchen.

Take the coins out of your wallet. Give them to your child. Let him create designs with them.

Home is where the hill is

Poof! You just became an ant. It's morning and you're waking up in your underground home. You decide you're going to visit all of your underground friends. Who will you say *"Hi"* to?

How many different noises can you make with your mouth? Experiment, you'll be amazed!

What would you do if this happened to you? *"You are riding your bike and you fall off of it as you're going around the corner?"*

What can you put in a wagon?

Why do you think it is so much fun to eat watermelon? What do you like about eating watermelon?

Where can you find water?

Close your eyes, look for a picture, tell someone else what you see.

What things could you do if you had very long fingernails at the end of each of your fingers?

Think about all of the different soaps in your house. What do you use them for?

There's a long flight of stairs. No one is on them. You could walk up the stairs, but you want to move up in a different way. How could you move to the top?

If a kangaroo wore clothes, what would he wear?

What animals can you think of that are green?

How does a pet invite you to play with him?

Pretend you're on a trip and you need to clean your face. How many ways can you do it?

Enjoy reading the book *It Looked Like Spilt Milk* by Charles Shaw. After this, go outside, lie down on the grass, look up at the clouds and find the shapes, creatures, animals, and people hiding among the clouds.
EXTENSION: Next time that you spill milk, look at the puddle before you clean it up.

What presents would you like to receive if today was your birthday?

What toppings can you put on hot dogs?

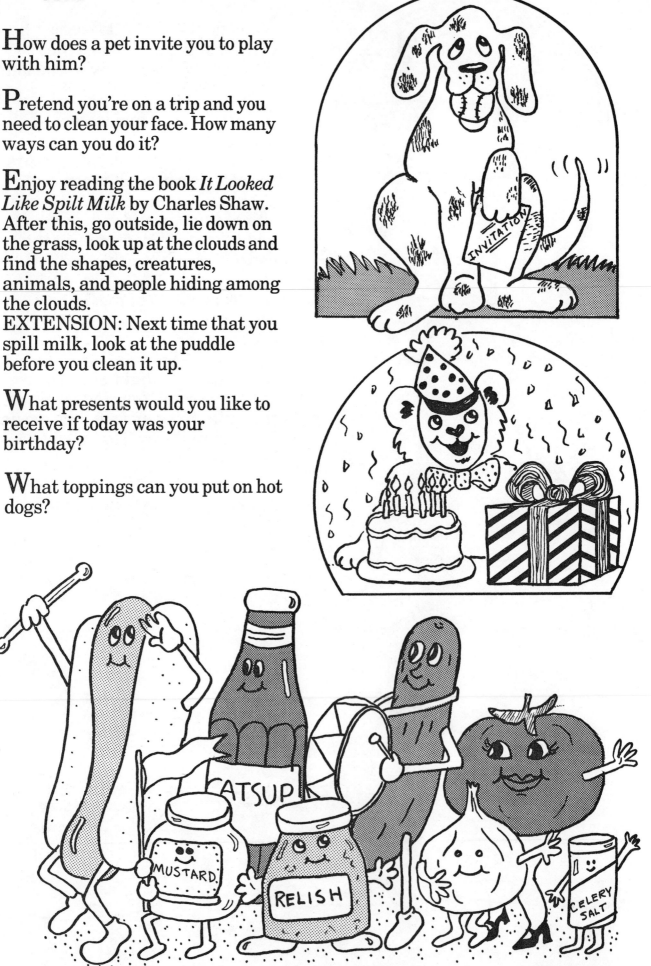

What vehicles move on the road?

Read this rhyme and then talk about other sounds which have a special meaning.

SIRENS

When the siren blows,
It seems to say,
"Clear the street,
Get out of the way."
Dick Wilmes

Popsicles keep you cool during the summer. You can make your own popsicles by freezing different liquids. What kinds of popsicles would you like to make? EXTENSION: Choose one kind and make it early in the morning so it will be ready for your afternoon treat.

What types of shoes do you have?

JULY

You want to dig a deep hole in the sand but you forgot your shovel. What else could you use? Keep thinking!!

What do you do at the beach?

If you wanted to fill balloons with air plus other things, what would you put in them? Do you think any of your balloons would float once they were blown up?

What happens when you eat an ice cream cone? (A friend of ours, Emily, says that her and her sister Jillian's tongues get cold, their hands get sticky, and would you believe they grow white mustaches within minutes.)

What do you eat for snacks?

What merry-go-round character do you like best? Why?

AUGUST

If you go exploring at the beach, what would you find?

Besides in your bed, where else could you sleep?

AUGUST

Who's in a parade?

Name all of the places you have been where you threw away trash.

How can you make 'your baby' happy?

What are all of the things you can do on a field?

Jiggle your body in as many ways as you can while keeping your head in the same place.

What happens when you cut your finger?

Sit quietly in the park. What noises do you hear? Are they quiet or loud sounds?

What do you like to do at birthday parties?

It's so hot outside. What different ways can you think of to stay cool?

Water is good for many things. How do you have fun in it?

What do you talk about with your stuffed toys?

What can you buy from a vending machine?

What would it be like to live on the sun?

Fruit kabobs are varieties of fruit cut up and put on toothpicks. They are refreshing on warm days. What types of fruit could you put on fruit kabobs?

What do you do on camping trips? Do you sit around the campfire like the people in this rhyme? What else do you do?

BY THE CAMPFIRE

We sat around the campfire
On a chilly night,
Telling spooky stories
In the pale moonlight.

Then we added some more logs
To make the fire bright,
And sang some favorite camp
* songs*
Together with all our might.

And when the fire flickered
And embers began to form,
We snuggled in our sleeping bags
All cozy, tired, and warm.

                    Dick Wilmes

AUGUST

Pretend you're the boss of a big zoo. You want to give everyone who buys popcorn an extra treat. You're going to put a toy in each bag. What kinds of toys would you use? Personally I'd like to find a plastic giraffe in my bag of popcorn.

You want to go up and down a hill lots of times, but each time you want to move in a different way. How many ways can you think of? I know two—I'd roll down then 'fly' back up. Next, I'd wiggle down and walk backwards to the top. I bet you'll think of lots more.

Where are all the places that you could find sand?

When do you huff and puff?

Give your child some sponges for the bathtub. Let him play.

Picnics are fun. Plan what you would put in your picnic basket.

You can put ice cream in a cone, in a bowl—what else?

What can you haul in a dump truck?

What games would you play if you had a pig for a pet?

What do you use rags for?

Play 'ZAP.' Snap your fingers and say *"Zap, I wish I were _____."* Let each person take a turn. Go around again and again.

If you were a porpoise, what tricks would you like to do?

What flies?

Dad's angry. Why?
EXTENSION: Use this rhyme to discuss times when you have other feelings.

FEELINGS

Smile when you're happy,
Cry when you are sad,
Giggle if it's funny,
Frown if you're mad.
                    Dick Wilmes

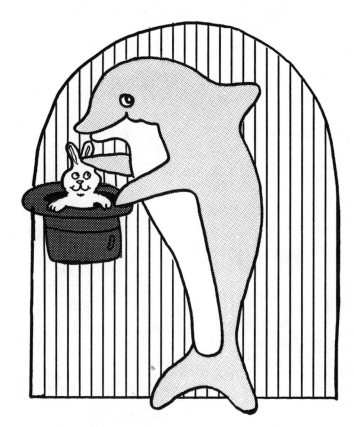

AUGUST

Pretend you're outside and you want to get into your house but the door is locked. How are you going to get in? Can you think of another way? Another? (Hope you never get locked out for real, but if you do you'll know just what to do!)

What can you do with dirt? EXTENSION: Enjoy this rhyme and discover how nature uses dirt.

DIRT

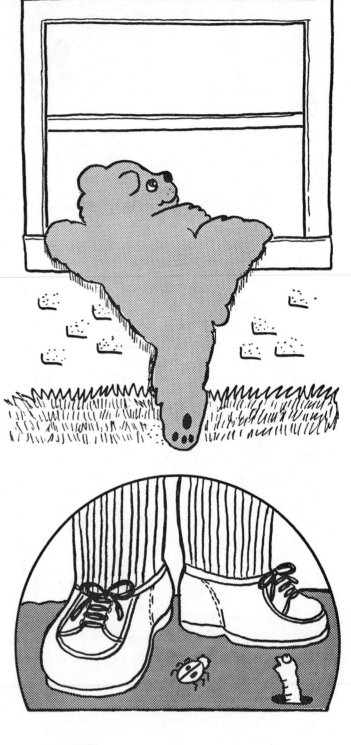

Dirt comes in colors,
Black, red, and brown.
It makes a home for animals,
Living in the ground.

Worms, snakes, ants, and bugs
Live beneath my shoe.
If there wasn't dirt between us
I wouldn't know what to do.

Dirt helps the tree to stand
Stately green and tall.
If it wasn't for our friend the dirt
I'm sure those trees would fall.

Dirt feeds the plants you know,
Minerals and nutrients too.
I think I'll eat my vegetables,
And leave the dirt for you!
                              Dick Wilmes

Name as many animals as you can that are shorter than you.

60

SEPTEMBER

HOLIDAYS

LABOR DAY celebrates the workers of the United States. As you're walking around, look for people who are working. What jobs are they doing?

Encourage your child to talk about jobs he'd like to do when he grows up. After discussing them with him, ask him to pick his favorite one for right now, knowing that he might change his mind.

Read this rhyme and talk about all of the firefighter's duties.

THE FIRE STATION

The fire station's empty,
There's no one there today.
Do you think they're on vacation
Or just gone out to play?
"NOOOOOO"

The big red doors are open
The fire trucks aren't there.
The ambulance is leaving now,
Their sirens fill the air.

I know they're at a fire.
I saw the trucks go past,
With sirens screaming loudly,
Their red and blue lights flashed.

They're racing to the Miller Barn,
There's a fire in the hay,
They'll use their water hoses,
And then they'll drive away.
                    Dick Wilmes

FIRST DAY OF SCHOOL brings many new adventures.

What do you think is going to happen during your first day of school?

What do you do to get ready for school?

What do you carry in your school bag?

GRANDPARENT'S DAY honors older people in our lives.

Your grandparents have a problem. You are visiting them for a day. They are trying to decide where to take you for an afternoon trip. Where would you enjoy going with your grandparents or older friends?

Tell me about your grandma/grandpa or another older friend you have.

MEXICAN INDEPENDENCE DAY is a Mexican
holiday celebrating independence from the Spanish. It is celebrated with parades, fireworks, and friends. Name all of the people and things you see in a parade.

JOHNNY APPLESEED DAY features an American
folk hero. In the legend of Johnny Appleseed it is said that he wore a tin pan on his head. What kinds of hats can you wear?
EXTENSION: Read *Caps For Sale* by Esphyr Slobodkina.

Read this rhyme to your child and figure out what might have happened to the apple after it fell on the person's head.

OUCH

*Apple green, apple red
An apple fell upon my head.*
Dick Wilmes

FIRST DAY OF FALL begins the season when leaves
change color and fall from the trees. Other than leaves, what falls quietly when dropped?

Rake! Rake! Rake up all of those fallen leaves. Now they're in a pile. What are you going to do with them?

What can you do with a brown paper lunch bag?

Name all of the yellow vegetables you can think of.

Read the story *Brown Bear, Brown Bear, What Do You See* by Bill Martin to your child. Soon after, let him pretend he is a brown bear. Say to him, *"Brown bear, brown bear what do you see?"* He can respond, *"I see a table looking at me."* Continue *"Brown bear, brown bear what else do you see?"* He responds again. After four or five responses go back and say, *"Brown bear, tell me everything you've seen so far."* Continue.

What can you think of to stuff celery with?
EXTENSION: Try some of your ideas. In fact, pick one and make it for tonight.

What does a spider web look like?

If you could plan the whole dinner, what would you have to eat? Remember dessert.

What types of animals are there on a merry-go-round?

When eating out, let your child choose what to eat for himself and then let him order it.

What do babies do all day long?

How many ways can you spread jelly on your sandwich?

When a child gives you a 'hug', say *"You're telling me that you love me. Can you tell me that you love me in another way?"* Encourage him by saying, *"I'll tell you I love you in another way."* Then give the child a kiss. Continue thinking of other ways.

How do you know when your mom's upset?

SEPTEMBER

If you could be any animal you wanted to be, which one would you pick? Why?

Let him choose all of his own clothes today.

Think of all of the ways you can move your body.

How do you say *"Hi"* to friends?

If you walked into a room and met a person who looked and acted just like you, what would you say to him?

I'm soooooooo happy when

_____.

Name the types of animals that live in your neighborhood.

Think of all of the ways a dog is like a cat. Is not like a cat.

What fruits and vegetables can you think of that have different colored skins and 'insides'?

OCTOBER

HOLIDAYS

COLUMBUS DAY commemorates the day Christopher Columbus landed in the Americas. If you were on one of Columbus' ships and you ran out of food, what would you do?

Make a telescope with your child. (Get a paper towel roll. Let him decorate it with markers. Punch a hole on each side of one end and loop a piece of string through it so your child can wear it around his neck.) Look through it and talk about all of the things he sees.

HALLOWEEN is a day of pretending. Pretend you're a witch. What would you like to do?

Take a Halloween Walk. Before the walk, talk about different Halloween characters and how they move. Start with bats which fly, scarecrows that flop, and so on. Once you've created your different characters, pretend that you are one and take a walk around the neighborhood. Halfway through the walk, pick another character and continue.

Once you've carved your pumpkin, what can you do with your seeds?

What materials can you use to change a pumpkin into a jack-o-lantern?

What types of costumes can you think of?

You have a friend named Spooky. Listen to his problem. *"Hi, I'm Spooky the ghost and I have a problem. I hope that you will help me solve it. When I go to children's homes on Halloween, they are always afraid of me. I am really a nice ghost. How can I make them like me?"*

Think of all of the things that the strong fall winds can blow around.

What do people do at gas stations?

If you put clown make-up on your face, what would you look like?

A boy and his dog are sitting under a tree on a gorgeous fall day. What are they saying to each other?

How many ways can you wiggle your toes?

When do you cry?

CRYING

Sometimes I cry when I'm angry
Sometimes when I'm sad
Or hurt or tired
Or hungry or sick
Or whenever I'm feeling bad.

My parents cry for the same
  reasons
And another reason too
They cry when they are happy
I can't understand that! Can you?
              Dick Wilmes

69

OCTOBER

Take a walk around the neighborhood. Look for squares and rectangles in the buildings. Next time look for triangles and then circles.

What parts of your body move when you walk?

What are pockets for? EXTENSION: Read *Katy No-Pocket* by Emmy Payne.

Read this rhyme and then remember all of the chores you do around your house. I help around my house by _____
_____.

EVENING CHORES

The dishes need washing,
Mother and I are a team.
She washes, I wipe them
Until they all gleam.

Dad and sister are helping.
They're sweeping the floors.
We all work together,
When doing the chores.
                    Dick Wilmes

After the wash is done, let your child match his socks.

What do squirrels do?

Look through a window near you? What do you see?

What games does 'your baby' like to play?

Make omelettes for dinner. Let every member of the family choose what 'insides' he wants.

Change your face in one way. For example, blow air into your cheeks or close one eye. Look at someone and let him figure out how you are changing your face.

Have fun with a piece of string.

What scares you? Why?

OCTOBER

What foods does your family like?

What things do you spread peanut butter on? Think of other things peanut butter would be good on.

What's the same about living on a farm and in the city?

Wiggle your mouth in as many ways as you can. If possible, do it in front of a mirror. You'll get lots of good laughs.

How many ways do you prepare potatoes?

If you were going to get dressed in a 'silly' way, what would you wear?

Exercise your tongue. Move it in and out quickly. What other exercises can you think of? Try them.

What animals live in the woods?

NOVEMBER

HOLIDAYS

THANKSGIVING gives people a time to reflect on their gifts. How do you show someone that you are thankful for all that they have done for you?

If you were going to a new land where there were no homes, where could you sleep?

Fill a horn of plenty. What fruits and vegetables would you put in your horn? Do you have a favorite fruit? Vegetable? What are they?

Say a Thanksgiving word such as 'turkey.' What words come to your mind when you think of a turkey? Enjoy this rhyme.

RUN FAST LITTLE TURKEY

The brave little Pilgrim
Went out in the wood
Looking for a meal
That would taste really good.

First she picked cranberries
Out in the bog.
Then she saw a turkey
Hiding in a log.

Run fast little turkey.
Run fast as you may.
Or you'll come to dinner
On Thanksgiving Day.
                    Dick Wilmes

NOVEMBER 1 Draw a simple turkey without feathers. Let your child cut out 30 colored feathers. Each day in November have him tell you one thing he is thankful for, likes, or is important to him. Write it on a feather. Let him glue the feather to the turkey. At the end of the month the turkey will have his full plumage.

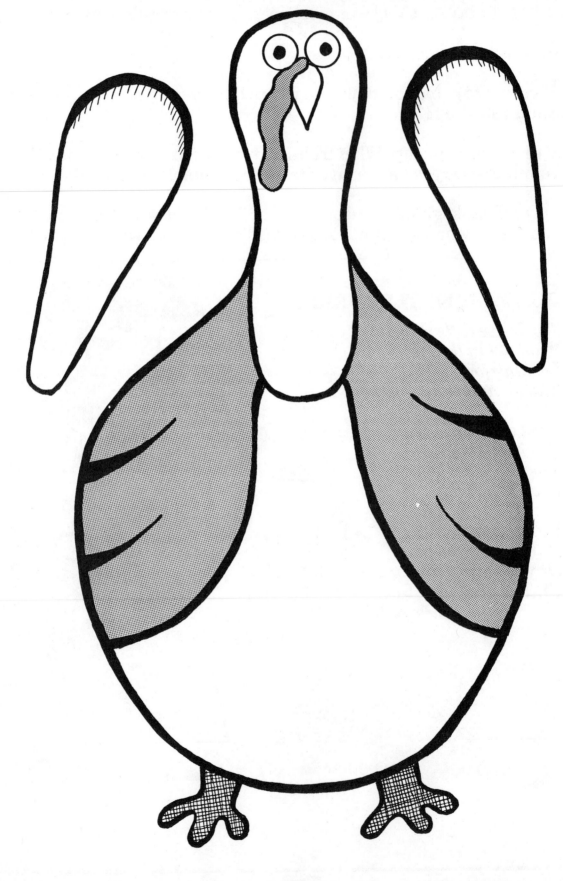

You're going to put pieces of fruit on the table. What can you put them in so they do not roll around? Maybe a pretty box. What else?

Do you like to play outside or inside better? Why?

What is the same about you and a robot?

What things do you really like about your family?

If you could fly through the air like a bird, what do you think you would see?

What decorations can you put on a cake?

What do you do in school?

What body parts can you move? Which ones don't move?

Name as many musical instruments as you can. *"Let's see, there's a drum, a violin, a _____.*

NOVEMBER

Think of different ways you can use your body to make music or keep rhythm. Then enjoy this rhyme.

THE BODY BAND

Beat, beat with your feet,
We're playing the body band.

Strum, strum with your thumb,
It's the best one in the land.

Clap, clap on your lap,
Keep rhythm with your knees.

Hear, hear with your ear,
Stop laughing if you please.

Cluck, cluck like a duck,
It's fun on a rainy day.

Pop, pop on your top,
Keep humming as you play.

Moan, moan all alone,
You're playing your solo now.

Haste, haste with your waist,
It's time to take your bow!
Dick Wilmes

Name all of the types of bread you can think of.
EXTENSION: Make a new type or buy one at the bakery.

76

Why do you think a turtle moves so slowly?

What days does your family celebrate?

Name the different parts of a car.

What are different ways to snuggle? Try them.

You're going to visit Grandma and Grandpa (or some good friends). What do you think will happen while you're there?

Look at a star and make a wish. EXTENSION: Sing 'Twinkle, Twinkle Little Star.'

Why do you eat?

Think of all of the large machines in your house. Tell someone else what they are.

What do cows do all day long?

NOVEMBER

If you took a walk through the woods, what animals would you see?

Two hands can clap. What else can they do?

On your way to school look for cars that are the same color.

Look carefully at a colorful pattern, say on a piece of wallpaper or material. Find all of the colors. How many were there? Are you sure you found them all?

What foods have a round shape? Can you think of any with a triangle shape?

What would you do if you could be invisible?

When a baby babbles, what kinds of things does he say?

If you were a dinosaur, what types of games would you play?

DECEMBER
HOLIDAYS

ST. NICHOLAS DAY honors a man born in Europe, who gave gifts to children. St. Nicholas liked to put the little surprises in people's shoes. Pretend you're St. Nick. What gifts would fit in shoes?

EXTENSION: What would you like St. Nick to leave in your shoe?

How is St. Nicholas going to carry all of the gifts he will give away?

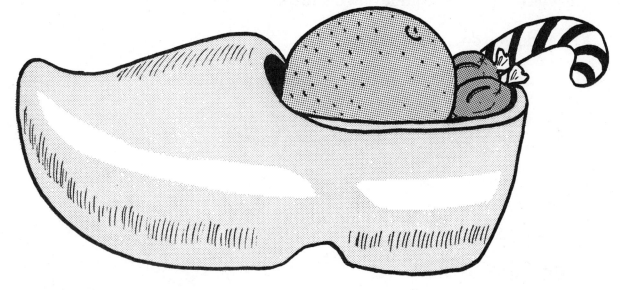

HANUKKAH is a Jewish festival of lights. Look carefully at the flames burning on the candles of the Menorah. What colors do you see in the flames?

What gifts would you like to receive during Hanukkah?

To whom do you give gifts during Hanukkah?

FIRST DAY OF WINTER begins the season of cold, snowy weather. Read *The Big Snow* by Hader and Hader. Talk about the different ways the animals have gotten ready for the winter season.

What do people do to prepare for the winter weather?

What clothes do you wear in winter? Why?

Going through a toy store? Look at all of the types of sleds. Which one would you like to slide down a hill on? Why?

What do you do in the snow?

What would you do if a snowperson came to visit you?

In the winter, most trees are bare except for the snow. What would you do if you walked outside and saw a tree filled with lollipops?

CHRISTMAS is a Christian holiday celebrating the birth of Jesus. If you were going to Jesus Christ's birthday party, what would you bring Him?

Jesus was born in a stable. What/who else was in the stable with Jesus that day?

What colors do you see on your Christmas tree?

Make a large Santa face. Divide the beard into 24 sections. Hang it on a wall. Beginning with #1, have your child glue a cotton ball on a number each day. As he does, have him think of a gift he would like for the holiday or a gift he thinks another member of the family would like.

DECEMBER

Think about all of the things that happen to popcorn kernels while they are in the popper. Now enjoy this rhyme.

THE POPCORN KERNEL

I am a popcorn kernel,
On the electric range,
With oil to my ankles,
Waiting for the change.

Pop, pop it's started happening,
The noise has just begun.
Pop, pop, there it goes again.
It sounds like lots of fun.

Explosions to the left of me.
Explosions to the right.
I'm just about to blow my top,
I really think I might.
BANG!!!!

Dick Wilmes

There are so many different types of brushes. Name every type you can think of. Start with your toothbrush. After you have thought and thought, read the rhyme. Did it help you remember several more?

BRUSHES IN MY HOME

The brushes in my home
Are simply everywhere.
I use them for my teeth each day,
And also for my hair.

We use them in the kitchen sink
And in the toilet bowls.
For putting polish on my shoes,
And to waterproof the soles.

Brushes are used to polish the
  floors,
And also paint the wall,
To clean the charcoal barbeque,
It's hard to name them all.

Dick Wilmes

Make holiday sandwiches as a special treat for your child's class. The afternoon before your child takes the treat to school, you and your child prepare it. First, using holiday cookie cutters, cut the bread. Then spread cream cheese or another type of spreadable cheese on the bread. Let your child decorate each sandwich with pieces of vegetables and nuts. Arrange them on a tray, cover tightly, and you're all set.

What types of wrappings can you wrap presents in?

What things do you do to take care of babies?

On the holidays you receive many cards. What could you do with them?
EXTENSION: Let your child pick one and then let him do it.

Tell a friend about your favorite toy.

After a commercial for a toy your child wants has played on a television program that you and he are watching, talk about the toy. Why does he want it? What does he know about it? What color is it?
EXTENSION: Next time you're in the store, look for the toy. Does it look like the toy portrayed on television? How? After looking at it, does he still want it?

DECEMBER

If you were holding a Raggedy Ann doll, what games would you like to play with her?

How many types of body movements do you use to communicate what you're trying to say?

What's red? Blue? Yellow?

How many ways can you wiggle your fingers?

Square, square, what is square?

What does your body do when you laugh? Think of your face, your stomach, your legs, and so on.

When two people hug, what could they be telling each other?

Some friends are coming over to visit. What will you play?

How many ways can you light up a room?

What do you like about your stuffed toys?

What do you do when you see a new snowfall?

FOR EVERY MONTH

an important resource for child care professionals

BUILDING BLOCKS

TAKE A LOOK AT BUILDING BLOCKS NEWSPAPER

PUBLISHED:
10 times a year with expanded editions in November/December and May/June.

RATES:
Family Edition: $10.00
Child Care Edition: $15.00

FOR A SAMPLE ISSUE
SEND YOUR NAME, ADDRESS (INCLUDING ZIP CODE) AND $2.00 TO:

BUILDING BLOCKS
38W567 Brindlewood
Elgin, Illinois 60123

CHILD CARE EDITION

BUILDING BLOCKS **Child Care Edition** offers early childhood professionals a total curriculum resource. It is divided into two parts. The first part is a potpourri of monthly ideas, activities, and information for you to use in your classroom as well as share with your parents. It is hand-lettered and charmingly illustrated.

The second part of the **Child Care Edition** features a different unit each issue. Included in each unit are:

- LEARNING CENTER SUGGESTIONS
- CIRCLE TIME ACTIVITIES
- ART IDEAS
- MUSIC, FINGERPLAYS AND ACTIVE GAMES
- EASY RECIPES
- ROUTINE TIME ACTIVITIES

BUILDING BLOCKS also offers a **Family Edition** which consists of the hand-lettered and illustrated portion.

The Circle Time Book

by Liz and Dick Wilmes

The Circle Time Book captures the spirit of seasons and holidays. The big book is filled with more than 400 circle time activities for the preschool classroom. Thirty-nine seasons and holidays are included.

A useful companion to **Everyday Circle Times.**

ISBN 0-943452-00-7, Building Blocks, 128 pages $8.95

Everyday Circle Times

by Liz and Dick Wilmes

Over 900 ideas for Circle Time. This is one of the most important and challenging periods in the children's day. Choose activities from 48 different units. Each unit is introduced with an opening activity, and expanded through language and active games, fingerplays, stores, recipes, books and more.

ISBN 0-943452-01-5, Building Blocks, 216 pages $12.95

Felt Board Fun

by Liz and Dick Wilmes

Make your felt board come alive. Discover how versatile it is as the children become involved with the wide range of activities designed to help them think creatively and learn basic concepts.

This unique book contains over 150 ideas with accompanying patterns.

ISBN 0-943452-02-3, Building Blocks, 224 pages $12.95

Gifts, Cards, Wraps

by Liz Wilmes and Dawn Zavodsky

Help the children sparkle with the excitement of gift-giving. **Gifts, Cards and Wraps** is filled with thoughtful gifts, unique wraps, and special cards which the children can make and give. Use the ideas for year 'round gift-giving to surprise moms, dads, grandparents, brothers, sisters, and other special friends. They're sure to bring smiles!

ISBN 0-943452-06-6, Building Blocks, 104 pages $7.95

Parachute Play

by Liz and Dick Wilmes

Now a year-round approach to one of the most versatile pieces of large muscle equipment. Starting with the basic techniques, **Parachute Play** provides you with over one hundred activities to make your parachute or a large bed sheet come alive for the children in your group.

ISBN 0-943452-03-1, Building Blocks, 96 pages $7.95

Exploring Art

by Liz and Dick Wilmes

Create it — Display it — Enjoy it — the secret to enhancing your children's art experience. **Exploring Art** features a variety of easy art activities for each month. Every idea is coordinated with an introductory activity, a display suggestion, and extension activities for expanding art into the curriculum. Over 250 art ideas in all, along with more than 500 related activities.

ISBN 0-943452-05-8, Building Blocks, 256 pages $16.95

Classroom Parties

by Susan Spaete

Laugh, play, and learn together as you and the children take a break from the normal routine to celebrate special days, holidays, and just silly events. Each party plan suggests decorations, trimmings, and snacks which the children can easily make to help set a festive mood. Choose from games, songs, art activities, stories, and other related experiences which will add to the excitement and fun. Everyone will leave with a smile on his face and fond memories of this occasion.

ISBN 0-943452-07-4, Building Blocks, 120 pages $8.95

Parent Programs and Open Houses

by Susan Spaete

Parent Programs and Open Houses is filled with a wide variety of year 'round presentations, pre-registration ideas, open houses, and end-of-the-year gatherings. Each of the programs involve the children from the beginning planning stages through the actual event. They are simple, short, and child-centered. Try them. Everyone will have a good time!

ISBN 0-943452-08-2, Building Blocks, 152 pages $9.95

ORDER FORM

NAME _____

ADDRESS _____

CITY _____

STATE _____ ZIP _____

QTY		EACH	TOTAL
_____	THE CIRCLE TIME BOOK	$ 8.95	_____
_____	EVERYDAY CIRCLE TIMES	$12.95	_____
_____	FELT BOARD FUN	$12.95	_____
_____	EXPLORING ART	$16.95	_____
_____	IMAGINATION STRETCHERS	$ 6.95	_____
_____	PARACHUTE PLAY	$ 7.95	_____
_____	GIFTS, CARDS & WRAPS	$ 7.95	_____
_____	CLASSROOM PARTIES	$ 8.95	_____
_____	PARENT PROGRAM & OPEN HOUSES	$ 9.95	_____
		TOTAL	_____

AVAILABLE FROM BOOKSTORES, SCHOOL SUPPLY STORES
OR ORDER DIRECTLY FROM:

BUILDING BLOCKS

38W567 Brindlewood, Elgin, Illinois 60123
312-742-1013   800-233-2448